# DOLLAR STORE DANNY
## and the Magic Mirror

# An AudioCraft Publishing, Inc. book

This book is a work of fiction. Names, places, characters and incidents are used fictitiously, or are products of the author's very active imagination.

Book storage and warehouses provided by *Chillermania* ©
Indian River, Michigan

No part of this published work may be reproduced in whole or in part, by any means, without written permission from the publisher. For information regarding permission, contact: AudioCraft Publishing, Inc., PO Box 281, Topinabee Island, MI 49791

Dollar $tore Danny and the Magic Mirror
Copyright © 2021 by Johnathan Rand/AudioCraft Publishing, Inc.
ISBN: 978-1-942950-01-1

**Librarians/Media Specialists:**
PCIP/MARC records available **free of charge** at
www.americanchillers.com

Illustrations by Michal Jacot © 2019 AudioCraft Publishing, Inc.
Cover/interior layout and graphics design by Howard Roark

DOLLAR $TORE DANNY © is copyright 2018 by AudioCraft Publishing, Inc. AMERICAN CHILLERS® , MICHIGAN CHILLERS® and FREDDIE FERNORTNER, FEARLESS FIRST GRADER® are
registered trademarks of AudioCraft Publishing, Inc.
All rights reserved.

Printed in USA

# The Magic Mirror

## WORLD HEADQUARTERS FOR BOOKS BY JOHNATHAN RAND!

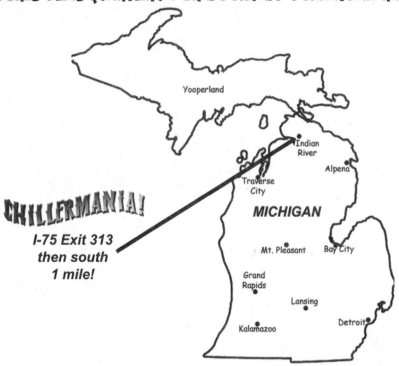

Visit the HOME for books by Johnathan Rand! Featuring books, hats, shirts, bookmarks and other cool stuff not available anywhere else in the world! Plus, watch the American Chillers website for news of special events and signings at **CHILLERMANIA** with author Johnathan Rand! Located in northern lower Michigan, on I-75! Take exit 313 . . . then south 1 mile! For more info, visit www.americanchillers.com or call (231) 238-0338. And be afraid! Be veeeery afraaaaaaiiiid . . . .

# Chapter One

Danny and his mother went to the dollar store.

"Danny," his mother said, "do not go far. We will not be here very long."

"Okay, Mom," Danny said.

Danny liked shopping at the dollar store. He always found fun things.

Today, he found an ordinary mirror.

He picked it up and looked at himself.

"Now, there is a good-looking kid," he said to himself in the mirror. He smiled. "It's like there are two of me."

The boy in the mirror winked! It was very strange.

The boy in the mirror winked at Danny again.

Danny scratched his head.

The boy in the mirror did not scratch his head.

"This is very strange," Danny said.

Suddenly, the boy jumped out of the mirror!

Danny gasped.

Standing in front of him was another boy that looked just like Danny!

# Chapter Two

Danny looked at the boy. The boy looked at him. He was wearing the same cap as Danny. He was wearing the same shirt, and the same pants and shoes.

"You look just like me," Danny said.

"And you look just like me," the other Danny said.

"Are you my brother?" Danny asked.

"I don't think so," the boy said.

"How did you get out of the mirror?" Danny asked.

The other Danny shrugged. "I don't know," he said. "But let's have some fun! Come on!"

Danny returned the mirror to the shelf. He followed the boy that looked like him. The two boys stopped. On the shelf were rows of plastic cups.

"Watch this," the other Danny said.

While Danny watched, the other boy (who looked very much like Danny) knocked all the cups off the shelf! They fell to the floor and bounced at Danny's feet.

"Hey!" Danny said to the other boy. "Don't do that!"

"It's fun!" the other Danny said.

"No," Danny said. "It's not." He looked at the plastic cups scattered on the floor. "You are making a mess."

"So?" the other boy said. "I look just like you. You are the one who will get in trouble."

Danny's eyes grew wide. He knew the other Danny was right!

Then, the other boy saw something.

"Watch what I'm going to do now," the other Danny said.

"Wait!" the real Danny cried.

But it was too late. The other boy was already reaching for a glass vase on the shelf!

# Chapter Three

While Danny watched, the other Danny (who was being very, very bad) grabbed the glass vase that was on the shelf.

"Be careful," Danny said.

"That's made out of glass. If you drop it, it will break."

"I know," the other Danny said. "That's why it will be so much fun!"

"But if it breaks," Danny said, "you will get into trouble."

The other Danny smiled. He shook his head. "I won't get into trouble," he said. He pointed at Danny. "You will."

Danny gasped. He knew the other Danny was right.

"That's not very nice," Danny said.

"So?" the other Danny replied. "Watch this!"

Danny watched. The other Danny reached back with the vase . . . and threw it into the air! It was going to smash into a million pieces!

# Chapter Four

Danny watched the vase go up, up, higher and higher.

It began to fall back down.

Danny threw up his hands.

The vase came down, down.

Danny caught it in his hands! He had been very lucky.

Danny put the vase on the shelf.

"There," he said. He looked at the other Danny. "Now, don't do that again."

The other Danny grinned. He shook his head. "I won't," he said. "This will be more fun."

"What?" Danny asked.

"You will see," the other Danny said. "Watch this."

While Danny watched, the other Danny reached out. On the shelf were rows and rows of glasses.

"No," Danny said to the other Danny. "Leave those glasses alone!"

"Too late!" the other Danny said. He reached out with his hand. "I'm going to knock all of them to the floor!"

Danny gasped. "No!" he cried. "Don't! Please!"

"This is going to be a lot of fun," the other Danny said.

"Please be nice," Danny said.

The other Danny did not hear him. He swung his arm and knocked the glasses from the shelf! They were going to shatter on the floor!

# Chapter Five

Danny could only watch as the glasses fell to the floor.

He placed his hands over his ears so he would not hear the glass breaking.

But the glasses did not break! Instead, they bounced!

They were only plastic!

Danny rushed to pick them up. He put them on the shelf.

"Rats," the other Danny said. He looked around. "Now what can I do?"

"Wait right there," Danny said. "Do not go anywhere."

Quickly, Danny ran to the other shelf and found the mirror. Then, he ran to the other Danny.

"Get back in here," Danny said. "Get back in the mirror where you belong."

"I have a better idea," the other Danny replied. "Watch this."

"What are you going to do?" Danny asked.

"Just watch," the other Danny replied.

At the end of the aisle was a metal basket with colorful pool noodles. The pool noodles were very long and made of foam. They looked like spears.

The other Danny pulled a blue pool noodle from the basket. He looked at it.

Then he looked around. Not far away, he saw a woman pushing a cart.

"Watch this," he said with an evil grin. "I'm going to throw this and hit that lady over there."

"That's my mom!" Danny cried. "Don't do that!"

Danny grabbed the pool noodle before the other Danny could throw it. He yanked it out of his hands as Danny's mother vanished around the corner.

"You are no fun at all," the other Danny said.

"I don't want to get into trouble," Danny said.

"Let's see," the other boy said. He reached up and stroked his chin with his fingers. "What else can we do for fun?"

Then, Danny heard another voice from the next aisle over.

"Danny? Where are you?"

It was his mother!

"I'm right over here, Mom!" Danny said. "I want you to meet someone."

The other Danny raised his eyebrows. "I've got to go," he said. "I don't want to get into trouble." Without another word, he jumped into the mirror. He was gone.

Danny's mother appeared.

"There you are," she said. "Why are you holding a mirror?"

"There was another Danny just like me!" Danny said. "He jumped out of this mirror and was trying to cause trouble."

Danny's mother smiled. "Where is he now?"

"He's back in the mirror," Danny said. He looked in the mirror. A boy stared back at him, but it was his own face. The other Danny was gone.

"Well," his mother said. "I need a new mirror. Let's buy that one and take it home."

On his way home in the car, he looked at the mirror. He wondered if the other Danny would ever come out again.

And he wondered what would happen the next time he and his mother went to the dollar store.

# The End

# ABOUT THE AUTHOR

Johnathan Rand has authored more than 100 books for children and adults since the year 2000, with over 6 million copies in print. His series include the incredibly popular *AMERICAN CHILLERS, MICHIGAN CHILLERS, FREDDIE FERNORTNER-FEARLESS FIRST GRADER, THE ADVENTURE CLUB, DOLLAR $TORE DANNY*, and the all-new *NIGHTMARE NATION* series. When not traveling, Rand lives in northern Michigan with his wife and adopted shelter dogs. He is also the only author in the world to have a store that sells only his works: <u>**CHILLERMANIA**</u> is located in Indian River, Michigan, and is open year round. Johnathan Rand is not always at the store, but he has been known to drop by frequently. Find out more at:

## WWW.AMERICANCHILLERS.COM

## OFFICIAL TRADING CARDS ARE HERE!

Collect cards for every book! Collectible cards are available for all *American Chillers, Michigan Chillers, Freddie Fernortner, Fearless First Grader* and *Dollar $tore Danny* series of books, including very rare and valuable special-issue limited edition World Premiere Platinum Cards! Find out how to get yours at **www.americanchillers.com**.

# CHECK OUT SOME OF THESE CHILLING,

#1: The Michigan Mega-Monsters
#2: Ogres of Ohio
#3: Florida Fog Phantoms
#4: New York Ninjas
#5: Terrible Tractors of Texas
#6: Invisible Iguanas of Illinois
#7: Wisconsin Werewolves
#8: Minnesota Mall Mannequins
#9: Iron Insects Invade Indiana
#10: Missouri Madhouse
#11: Poisonous Pythons Paralyze Pennsylvania
#12: Dangerous Dolls of Delaware
#13: Virtual Vampires of Vermont
#14: Creepy Condors of California
#15: Nebraska Nightcrawlers
#16: Alien Androids Assault Arizona
#17: South Carolina Sea Creatures
#18: Washington Wax Museum
#19: North Dakota Night Dragons
#20: Mutant Mammoths of Montana
#21: Terrifying Toys of Tennessee
#22: Nuclear Jellyfish of New Jersey
#23: Wicked Velociraptors of West Virginia
#24: Haunting in New Hampshire
#25: Mississippi Megalodon
#26: Oklahoma Outbreak
#27: Kentucky Komodo Dragons
#28: Curse of the Connecticut Coyotes
#29: Oregon Oceanauts
#30: Vicious Vacuums of Virginia
#31: The Nevada Nightmare Novel
#32: Idaho Ice Beast
#33: Monster Mosquitoes of Maine
#34: Savage Dinosaurs of South Dakota
#35: Maniac Martians Marooned in Massachusetts
#36: Carnivorous Crickets of Colorado
#37: The Underground Undead of Utah
#38: The Wicked Waterpark of Wyoming
#39: Angry Army Ants Ambush Alabama
#40: Incredible Ivy of Iowa
#41: North Carolina Night Creatures
#42: Arctic Anacondas of Alaska
#43: Robotic Rodents Ravage Rhode Island
#44: Arkansas Algae Monsters

**For best prices and complete selection of all titles in stock,**

# GREAT BOOKS BY JOHNATHAN RAND!

#1: Mayhem on Mackinac Island
#2: Terror Stalks Traverse City
#3: Poltergeists of Petoskey
#4: Aliens Attack Alpena
#5: Gargoyles of Gaylord
#6: Strange Spirits of St. Ignace
#7: Kreepy Klowns of Kalamazoo
#8: Dinosaurs Destroy Detroit
#9: Sinister Spiders of Saginaw
#10: Mackinaw City Mummies
#11: Great Lakes Ghost Ship
#12: AuSable Alligators
#13: Gruesome Ghouls of Grand Rapids
#14: Bionic Bats of Bay City
#15: Calumet Copper Creatures
#16: Catastrophe in Caseville
#17: A Ghostly Haunting in Grand Haven
#18: Sault Ste. Marie Sea Monsters
#19: Drummond Island Dogman
#20: Lair of the Lansing Leprechauns

## NIGHTMARE NATION
### THE STATE OF FEAR IS HERE

#1: Village of the Dolls
#2: Night of the Hodag

## THE ADVENTURE CLUB
#1: Ghost in the Graveyard
#2: Ghost in the Grand
#3: The Haunted Schoolhouse

## American Chillers Double Thrillers:
*Vampire Nation* &
*Attack of the Monster Venus Melon*

For Teens:
**PANDEMIA**: A novel of the
bird flu and the end of the world
*(written with Christopher Knight)*

#1: The Fantastic Flying Bicycle
#2: The Super-Scary Night-Thingy
#3: A Haunting We Will Go
#4: Freddie's Dog Walking Service
#5: The Big Box Fort
#6: Mr. Chewy's Big Adventure
#7: The Magical Wading Pool
#8: Chipper's Crazy Carnival
#9: Attack of the Dust Bunnies From Outer Space
#10: The Pond Monster
#11: Tadpole Trouble
#12: FrankenFreddie!
#13: Day of the Dinosaurs

## CREEPY CAMPFIRE CHILLERS VOLUME 1 & VOLUME 2

*(Spine-tingling audio stories written and read aloud by Johnathan Rand on two specially-priced compact discs!)*

#1: The Dangerous Dinosaur
#2: The Salt Shaker Spaceship
#3: The Crazy Crayons
#4: The Shampoo Shark Attack
#5: The Greeting Card Camping Trip
#6: The Magic Mirror

**order direct from the publisher at www.americanchillers.com**

All AudioCraft Publishing, Inc. books are proudly printed, bound, and manufactured in the United States of America, utilizing American resources, labor, and materials.